SOAR TO SUCCESS

THE INTERMEDIATE INTERVENTION PROGRAM

Student Guide

Level 3

Senior Author
J. David Cooper

Authors
Irene Boschken
Janet McWilliams
Lynne Pistochini

HOUGHTON MIFFLIN

Boston • Atlanta • Dallas • Geneva, Illinois • Palo Alto • Princeton

Design, Production, and Illustration: PiperStudiosInc

Printed in the U.S.A.

ISBN: 0-395-78131-0

89-WC-04 03 02 01 00 99

SOAR TO SUCCESS

Contents

SOAR TO SUCCESS

Name _____

REFLECTION

1 How do you think Melanie and Grandpa felt after Arthur "helped" them? Explain why.

_____

_____

_____

_____

REFLECTION

2 Do you think Arthur should be rewarded richly when he

does a task properly? _____ Why or why not?

_____

_____

_____

_____

_____

Name _____

REFLECTION

3

Circle the strategy you used most.

Strategy Box			
Predict	Clarify	Question	Summarize

Name at least one place where you used this strategy or modeled it for someone else. Write the page number(s).

_____

_____

_____

_____

How did this strategy help you?

_____

_____

_____

_____

Name _____

REFLECTION

1

Why do you think Arturo likes to conduct the orchestra?

_____

_____

_____

_____

_____

REFLECTION

2

Do you think Arturo should cancel the next concert and tour? Why?

_____

_____

_____

_____

_____

Name _____

3

Circle the strategy you used most.

Strategy Box			
Predict	Clarify	Question	Summarize

Name one place in the story where you used this strategy.

_____

_____

_____

Explain how this strategy helped.

_____

_____

_____

_____

_____

Name _____

REFLECTION

4 What did Arturo learn when he conducted without his baton?

_____

_____

_____

_____

_____

_____

The Wolf's Chicken Stew

Name _____

REFLECTION

1 What do you like to do more than anything else in the world?

_____

_____

_____

_____

REFLECTION

2 Why does the wolf decide not to catch the chicken right away?

_____

_____

_____

Name _____

REFLECTION

3

What would you do with all the food that the wolf bakes?

_____

_____

_____

_____

_____

Name _____

REFLECTION

4

Circle the strategy you used most in the story.

Strategy Box			
Predict	Clarify	Question	Summarize

On what page(s) did you use this strategy?

_____

_____

_____

How did this strategy help you?

_____

_____

_____

_____

Name _____

REFLECTION

1 Was it right for Harry to bring home the wounded bird?
Why do you think so?

_____

_____

_____

_____

_____

REFLECTION

2 Why do the birds follow Harry and stay
outside his window?

_____

_____

_____

_____

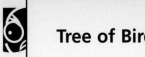

Name _____

REFLECTION

3

Circle the strategy you used most in this lesson.

Strategy Box			
Predict	Clarify	Question	Summarize

Where did you use this strategy?

_____

How did you use this strategy?

_____

_____

_____

_____

_____

Name _____

4

What did you like best about the story?

_____

_____

_____

_____

Why?

_____

_____

_____

_____

BIRD SEED

Animals in Winter

Name _____

REFLECTION

1

What does *migrate* mean?

_____

_____

_____

_____

_____

REFLECTION

2

Summarize how a woodchuck gets ready for winter.

_____

_____

_____

_____

Name _____

REFLECTION

3

Why do pikas cut more grass than they can eat in the summer?

_____

_____

_____

_____

REFLECTION

4

What animal interests you most in this book? Why?

_____

_____

_____

_____

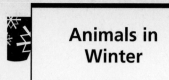 **Animals in Winter**

Name _____

Circle a strategy that helped you read this book.

Strategy Box			
Predict	Clarify	Question	Summarize

Find a place in the book where you used this strategy.

I used this strategy on page(s) _____.

_____

Tell how you used the strategy.

_____

_____

_____

_____

_____

Name _____

Story Map

Title

Setting

Characters

Problem

Major Events

Outcome

Name _____

REFLECTION

1 What is another way the stranger might pay for his meal?

_____

_____

_____

_____

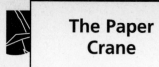

REFLECTION

2 Why would a dancing crane make people want to come to a restaurant?

_____

_____

_____

_____

REFLECTION

3 Would you like to eat a meal in this restaurant? Why or why not?

_____

_____

_____

_____

_____

_____

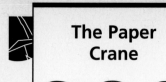

Name _____

REFLECTION

4

Circle the strategy you used most.

Strategy Box			
Predict	**Clarify**	**Question**	**Summarize**

Name at least one place where you used this strategy or modeled it for someone else. Write the page number(s).

_____

How did this strategy help you?

_____

_____

_____

_____

Name _____

REFLECTION

1

How are whales different from fish?

_____

_____

_____

_____

REFLECTION

2

Summarize how a whale breathes.

_____

_____

_____

_____

Name _____

3

What kinds of sounds do whales make?

_____

_____

_____

_____

Why do you think they make these sounds?

_____

_____

_____

_____

Name _____

REFLECTION

4

Circle the section you liked best in *Baby Whales Drink Milk.*

Pages 4–9 Whales are mammals.	**Pages 10–17** Newborn whales
Pages 18–23 Whales' temperature, blubber, and sounds	**Pages 24–32** Where whales live, what they eat

How did one of the four strategies help you read that section?

Predict

_____

_____

Clarify

_____

_____

Question

_____

_____

Summarize

_____

_____

A Bicycle for Rosaura

Name _____

Story Map

Title

Setting

Characters

Problem

Major Events

Outcome

Name _____

REFLECTION

1 Why does Rosaura the hen want a bicycle for her birthday?

_____

_____

_____

_____

REFLECTION

2 What would you do if you had to find a bicycle for a hen?

_____

_____

_____

_____

Name _____

3

What seems strange about the man who comes to the town?

_____

_____

_____

_____

_____

Name _____

REFLECTION

Circle the strategy you used most.

Strategy Box			
Predict	Clarify	Question	Summarize

Name at least one place where you used this strategy or modeled it for someone else. Write the page number(s).

_____

How did this strategy help you?

_____

_____

_____

_____

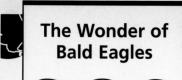

The Wonder of Bald Eagles

Name _____

1

Why do you think the bald eagle was chosen as a symbol of our country?

_____

_____

_____

_____

_____

2

Summarize how the bald eagle catches its prey.

_____

_____

_____

_____

_____

_____

Name _____

REFLECTION

3

Circle the strategy you used most.

Strategy Box			
Predict	**Clarify**	**Question**	**Summarize**

On what page (s) did you use this strategy?

I used the _____ strategy on

page(s) _____ .

How did this strategy help you?

_____

_____

_____

_____

_____

Name _____

REFLECTION

4

Why should people not get too close to a bald eagle's nest?

_____

_____

_____

_____

_____

REFLECTION

5

What can people do to help bald eagles?

_____

_____

_____

_____

Name _____

REFLECTION

1

What is waste?

_____

_____

_____

_____

_____

REFLECTION

2

Summarize what happens to waste at a landfill.

_____

_____

_____

_____

_____

Name _____

Circle the strategy you used most.

Strategy Box			
Predict	Clarify	Question	Summarize

Where did you use this strategy or model it for someone else?

I used the _____ strategy on

page (s) _____ .

How did this strategy help you?

The _____ strategy helped me

_____

_____

_____

_____

Name _____

REFLECTION

4

What household items do you use that might be made from recycled materials?

_____

_____

_____

_____

_____

REFLECTION

5

Why do you think the author wrote this book?

_____

_____

_____

_____

_____

_____

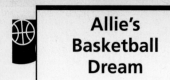

Allie's Basketball Dream

Name _____

Story Map

Title

Setting

Characters

Problem

Major Events

Outcome

Allie's
Basketball
Dream

Name _____

REFLECTION

1 Why did the boys laugh at Allie when she tried to play basketball?

_____

_____

_____

_____

REFLECTION

2 Would you respond to Allie's friends in the same way she did? Why or why not?

_____

_____

_____

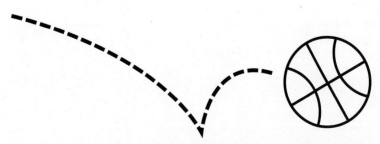

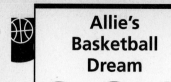

REFLECTION

3

What does Allie tell Buddy about girls playing basketball?

_____

_____

_____

_____

_____

_____

Name _____

REFLECTION

4 Circle the section you liked best in *Allie's Basketball Dream.*

Pages 4–9 Allie gets the basketball and begins to play	**Pages 10–17** Allie's friends won't play with her.
Pages 18–23 Buddy tries to trade with Allie.	**Pages 24–32** Allie begins to make baskets.

Choose a strategy that helped you read that section. Then explain how the strategy helped you.

Predict   **Clarify**   **Question**   **Summarize**

The _____ strategy helped me read

pages _____ because

_____

_____

_____

_____

Name _____

Semantic Map

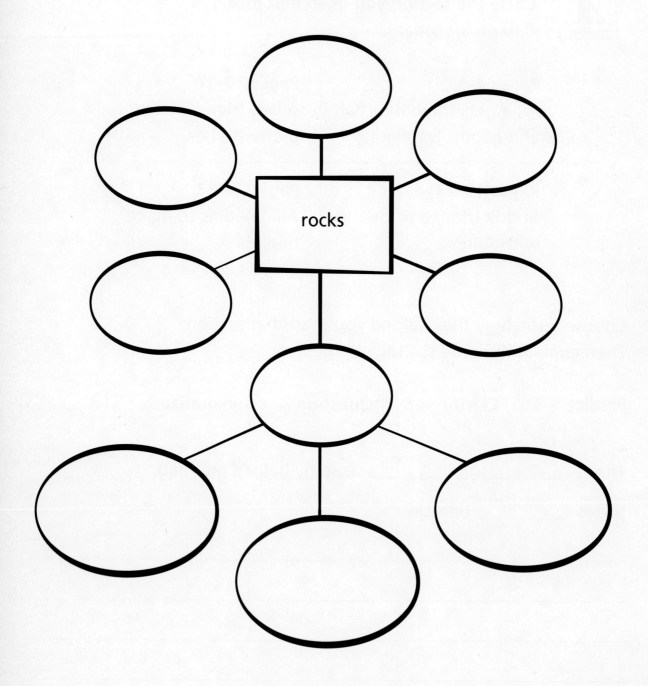

Name _____

REFLECTION

1

Why do some people collect rocks?

_____

_____

_____

_____

REFLECTION

2

What is igneous rock?

_____

_____

_____

_____

_____

Name _____

REFLECTION

3

Circle the strategy you used most.

Strategy Box			
Predict	Clarify	Question	Summarize

Name at least one place where you used this strategy or modeled it for someone else. Write the page number(s).

_____

How did this strategy help you?

_____

_____

_____

_____

_____

Name _____

REFLECTION

4

How does shale change into slate?

_____

_____

_____

_____

_____

REFLECTION

5

What kinds of things would you like to collect? Why?

_____

_____

_____

_____

_____

Name _____

Story Map

Title

Setting

Characters

Problem

Major Events

Outcome

Name _____

REFLECTION

1

Why do you think Marisol wants to have a dog?

_____

_____

_____

_____

REFLECTION

2

Why does Pancho stay near Marisol's house?

_____

_____

_____

_____

_____

_____

Name _____

REFLECTION

3

Why is Marisol worried about Pancho?

_____

_____

_____

_____

What would you do if you were Marisol?

_____

_____

_____

_____

_____

Name _____

REFLECTION

Circle the chapter you like best in *The Outside Dog.*

Chapter 1
Marisol Wants a Dog

Chapter 2
A Collar for Pancho

Chapter 3
The Search

Chapter 4
Pancho Saves the Day

Circle a strategy that helped you read that chapter.

Strategy Box			
Predict	Clarify	Question	Summarize

I used the _____ strategy to help me

_____

_____

_____

_____

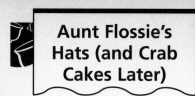

Name _____

REFLECTION

1 Why do Susan and Sarah love going to Aunt Flossie's house?

_____

_____

_____

_____

_____

REFLECTION

2 What does Aunt Flossie remember about the big Baltimore fire?

_____

_____

_____

_____

_____

Name _____

REFLECTION

3

Why does Aunt Flossie have a story for every one of her hats?

_____

_____

_____

_____

_____

REFLECTION

4

Which of Aunt Flossie's stories do you like best?

_____

Why do you like this story?

_____

_____

_____

_____

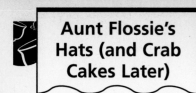

Name _____

5 Circle the section you liked best in *Aunt Flossie's Hats (and Crab Cakes Later)*.

The smoky green hat

The blue hat with a red feather

The favorite Sunday straw hat

How did one or more of the four strategies help you read that section?

Predict
_____

_____

Clarify
_____

_____

Summarize
_____

_____

Question
_____

_____

Name _____

K-W-L Chart

Title

What I **K**now	What I **W**ant to Find Out	What I **L**earned

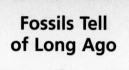

Name _____

My Notes to Clarify

Write any words or ideas that you need to clarify. Include
the page numbers.

Words or Ideas	Page
Pages 4–13 _____	_____
_____	_____
_____	_____
Pages 14–17 _____	_____
_____	_____
_____	_____
Pages 18–21 _____	_____
_____	_____
_____	_____
Pages 22–27 _____	_____
_____	_____
_____	_____
Pages 28–32 _____	_____
_____	_____

Name _____

REFLECTION

1

What is the fish fossil made of?

_____

_____

_____

_____

_____

_____

REFLECTION

2

Summarize how a dinosaur's footprint becomes a fossil.

_____

_____

_____

_____

_____

_____

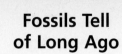

Name _____

REFLECTION

3

Circle the section you liked best so far in *Fossils Tell of Long Ago.*

Fossils of bones

Fossils of imprints

Fossils in ice and amber

How did one or more of the four strategies help you read that section?

Predict

_____

_____

Summarize

_____

_____

Clarify

_____

_____

Question

_____

_____

Name _____

REFLECTION

4

What can people learn from fossils?

_____

_____

_____

_____

_____

REFLECTION

5

What kind of fossil would you like to find? What would
you like to learn from it?

_____

_____

_____

_____

_____

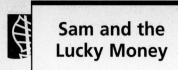

Name _____

My Notes to Clarify

Write any words or ideas that you need to clarify. Include the page numbers.

Words or Ideas	Page
Pages 2–9	
Pages 10–15	
Pages 16–21	
Pages 22–32	

Name _____

Story Map

Title

Setting

Characters

Problem

Major Events

Outcome

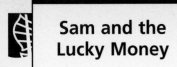

Name _____

1

How do you think Sam feels when he sees the old man with bare feet?

_____

_____

_____

_____

2

Why doesn't Sam buy any sweets in the bakery?

_____

_____

REFLECTION

3

Why does Sam feel angry in the toy store?

_____

_____

_____

_____

_____

How would you feel?

_____

_____

_____

_____

Name _____

REFLECTION

4

Circle the section you liked best in *Sam and the Lucky Money.*

Pages 2–9
Sam discovers the barefoot man.

Pages 10–15
Sam sees the lion.

Pages 16–21
Sam gets angry.

Pages 22–32
Sam gives money to the barefoot man.

How did one or more of the four strategies help you read that section?

Predict _____

_____

Clarify _____

_____

Summarize _____

_____

Question _____

_____

Name _____

My Notes to Clarify

Write any words or ideas that you need to clarify. Include the page numbers.

Words or Ideas	Page
Pages 3–9 _____	_____
_____	_____
_____	
Pages 10–21 _____	_____
_____	_____
_____	
Pages 22–29 _____	_____
_____	_____
_____	
Pages 30–39 _____	_____
_____	_____
_____	
Pages 40–46 _____	_____
_____	_____

Name _____

Event Map

Title

Event 1

Event 2

Event 3

Event 4

Event 5

Name _____

Clouds of Terror

REFLECTION

1 What did the children think about the cloud that they saw coming on the prairie?

_____

_____

_____

_____

REFLECTION

2 Why was it so important for the Lundstroms to get rid of the grasshoppers?

_____

_____

_____

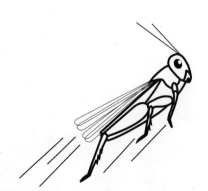

Clouds of Terror

Name _____

3

Circle the strategy you used most so far.

Strategy Box			
Predict	Clarify	Question	Summarize

Name at least one place where you used this strategy or modeled it for someone else. Write the page number(s).

_____

_____

How did this strategy help you?

_____

_____

_____

_____

Name _____

REFLECTION

4

Why did Mr. Lundstrom leave to work at the lumber camp?

_____

_____

_____

_____

REFLECTION

5

Do you think the Lundstrom family will continue to be able to survive on the prairie?

_____

_____

_____

_____

Name _____

My Notes to Clarify

Write any words or ideas that you need to clarify. Include the page numbers.

Words or Ideas	Page
Pages 1–11	
Pages 12–21	
Pages 22–30	
Pages 31–42	

Name _____

Story Map

Title

Setting

Characters

Problem

Major Events

Outcome

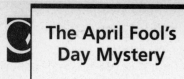

The April Fool's Day Mystery

Name _____

REFLECTION

1 Do you think Billy Wade put the snake in the flour bin? Why or why not?

_____

_____

_____

_____

_____

_____

_____

REFLECTION

2 Why did Kate believe the snake was in the flour bin long enough to get warm?

_____

_____

_____

_____

_____

Name _____

REFLECTION

3 Do you think Mickey and Kate are good detectives?
Why or why not?

_____

_____

_____

_____

_____

Would you like to be a detective? Why or why not?

_____

_____

_____

_____

_____

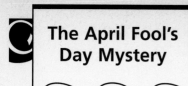

Name _____

REFLECTION

4 Circle the section you liked best in *The April Fool's Day Mystery.*

Chapters 1–2 "Puzzles and Pranks" and "A Real Private Eye"	**Chapters 3–5** "Sleuthing Snakes" to "Caught in the Library"
Chapters 6–7 "The scene of the Crime" and "What Mr. Butterfield Knows"	**Chapters 8–10** "What Suzy Didn't Know" to "The Case is Closed"

How did one or more of the four strategies help you read that section?

Predict

_____

_____

Clarify

_____

_____

Summarize

_____

_____

Question

_____

_____

Clarify/Phonics How to Say a Word

When I come to a word I don't know, first I look for chunks I know.

I know _____. If I still don't know the word, I look for letter

sounds. In this word, I know the sounds ____, ____, and ____. If I

blend the sounds together, the word is _____.

Finally, I check the meaning by rereading the sentence.

Clarify A Word Meaning

I read this word: _____. I'm not sure what this word

is or what it means. I look at the picture or read to the end of the

sentence. Now I think the word means . . .

Clarify An Idea

I don't understand this idea: _____.

First I _____ (reread, look at pictures, etc.). Then

I understand that. . . . I reread the sentence and it makes sense.

Predict

When I predict, I use clues from the pictures or from what I have read to help me figure out what will happen next (or what I will learn). I predict . . .

Question

When I question, I ask something that can be answered as I read or after I finish reading. I might ask . . .

Summarize

When I summarize, I tell in my own words the important things I have read.

Name _____

Book Log

Title	Author	Date Completed	Comments

Name _____

Book Log

Title	Author	Date Completed	Comments